WHO CONTROLS ME?

WHO CONTROLS ME?

A Psychotheological Reflection

Thomas A. Kane, Ph. D.

Foreword by ANNA POLCINO, M.D.

An Exposition-Collegium Book

EXPOSITION PRESS
HICKSVILLE, NEW YORK

NIHIL OBSTAT: William J. O'Halloran, S.J., Ph.D.

IMPRIMATUR: ✚   Bernard J. Flanagan, D.D., J.C.D.
                    Bishop of Worcester

FIRST EDITION

© 1974 by Thomas A. Kane

Library of Congress Catalog Card Number: 74-22261

ISBN 0-682-48186-6

Printed in the United States of America

To
MOTHER AND FATHER
with much gratitude

CONTENTS

FOREWORD by Anna Polcino   11

PREFACE   17

I.   *Who Controls Me?*   21

II.   *Identity and the Individual*   27

III.   *Personal Identity and Group Identity*   35

IV.   *Personal Identity and Social Change*   43

V.   *Oppression and Loss of Identity*   45

VI.   *Technology and False Identity*   49

VII.   *Revolution and the Recovery of Identity*   57

VIII.   *Identity, Social Change, and Religious Values*   65

IX.   *Affirmation and Identity*   71

BIBLIOGRAPHY   77

INDEX   79

"The concern for man and his destiny must always be the chief interest of all technical effort. Never forget it among your diagrams and equations."

—ALBERT EINSTEIN

FOREWORD

As a psychologist, educator, priest, and a truly human person, Thomas A. Kane brings a deep knowledge of human development and behavior in this study of the problems encountered by men and women who live in this present age of rapid change. His knowledge, combined with his broad experience in working with and talking to and treating many men and women of various walks of life, that is, of various professions, etc., has enabled him to evaluate objectively and with sensitivity the psychological strengths and weaknesses of life itself, and the various individuals who choose to ask the questions: "Who am I?" "Who are you?" "Where are you going?" "Where am I going?" In reality, he has combined all these questions into the one question "WHO CONTROLS ME?"

It is a relevant question to ask in this period of change or transition that society and various parts of the world are undergoing. There is a change in the world which is a source of confusion and unsettlement. In the process of adjustment of many individuals to these changes, each seems to lose one's sense of identity,

11

if only because the old habits and attitudes no longer fit neatly into the new pattern of environmental demands. This book is a profound and penetrating study of the identity crisis and its evolution, and of the development of the human person and society at large.

In the author's delineation of the controlling forces that influence us, we poignantly experience the confusion and doubt, the challenge of pain in adjusting to a new era. In this process of critical evaluation and adjustments that have to be made in the process of growth, it is to be expected that we shall experience a sense of loss, of being cut off from our safe moorings; in fact, even that we shall question our own identity and authenticity. And, as much as we may be convinced intellectually that such adaptations and changes are necessary, this does not lessen the anxiety and fear that each individual may experience in venturing into a new and as yet uncharted land.

If the development of personality is therefore a prerequisite to a meaningful life in society, it follows logically from the principle that love of self precedes love of others, both in the natural and supernatural order. One recognizes in Dr. Kane a concern for persons, a sensitivity to persons, and a respect for the individual along with the awareness of the weaknesses and fallibilities inherited in any human person. Our present generation demands a more integrated approach to the problems of human life. Even though great inroads into psychology and psychiatry have been made, many of the advances made by former authorities are

now being questioned because of a realization that the
spiritual aspect of man is most important in understanding the whole person. We are realizing more and more
that the problems of life are not sought in a one-dimen-
sional solution; we must bear upon a corporate understanding of the various sciences and other aspects of
human living to solve the problems of life.

Dr. Kane draws upon the insights of both theology
and psychology, and in combining both, arrives at a
psychotheological approach. He reflects on the experience of many of the great truths of our Judeo-Christian tradition; he qualifies that theological truths are
in essence intermingled and mutually illuminating. A
psychotheological approach to the problems of human
living is a source of nourishment for solution to these
problems. If society is to be healed and the identity of
each individual is to be assured, there must be an increase in awareness and need for an integrated development in human society; that is, a furthering of the
physical, mental, social, and spiritual development of
the whole man.

Healing is to be understood not only as an allevia-
tion of external pressures but also as a response to
man's search for internal liberation. Healing includes
going to the root cause of manifested problems by help-
ing bring about structure change; that is, by not letting
change control us but by our controlling the forces of
change, which aims at deeper personal liberation. It is
the task to which redemptive incarnation addresses
itself. In reality, healing is aimed at the development

of people in authentic diversity, accepting the individual where he is, and thus, we can say, as affirming that individual.

Healing can be seen in the context of today's situation and the thrust toward liberation that embraces man's aspirations and that struggles to free man not only from personal bondage but—even more important —from social bondage, from these products of our religio-cultural, political, economic systems. Healing ministry includes everyone, whether professional or not, and it is a ministry that draws on the faith dimension of an individual's commitment and reaches out to the community and to the society in which the individual finds himself. Healing of the whole man implies the healing not only of the physical but the mental, as well, and it cannot be separated from other activities that in some way or other are aimed at restoring man to his physical or spiritual wholeness. All such activities, whether on the individual, social, political, national, or international level—all are interrelated. They all strive for man's liberation, which, in fact, is none other than the freedom from all bonds that prevent him from developing into the mature and free man that he was to be, by God's design, and for which he was re-created by Christ.

Our strong desire should be affirming care to help restore man to his original wholeness and thus to contribute to his happiness. This means that we do not see persons as cases to be dealt with but as persons in need of our loving care. Who controls me? This brings us to the realization that the goal of man's life is not to lead him to the jealously autonomous possession of himself, but to bring him ultimately to a self-giving that is evermore consistent, free, fully human, and most nobly Christian.

This book, which discusses so truly and unambiguously the psychotheological problems encountered in our society, comes at a time when it is needed by many individuals. It is written in a language which is poetic and scholarly and, therefore, appealing to the intelligent, intuitive, and idealistic men and women of our times. It is a book that I recommend to anyone concerned. It is a book that is recommended to those who are searching for their own identity and authenticity, and therefore a book that will appeal to any man or woman in any state of life, whether he or she be a professional psychiatrist, or a housewife, for so many in all walks of life are searching for and questioning their identity in our present society.

ANNA POLCINO, M.D.
Former Medical Director
Holy Family Hospital
Karachi, West Pakistan;
Presently
Clinical Instructor in Psychiatry
University of Massachusetts Medical School

PREFACE

Some books are deliberately planned by the authors. Others seem merely to accumulate. This book falls into the latter category. My files began to grow as I put together articles, lectures, and workshop notes, until there was a stack of material that seemed to say, "Put me together." But the most recent motivation came from the group of graduate students who so eagerly responded to the content of my lectures during an academic tour in Great Britain.

Over the years there has been an increasing literature dealing with identity. For the most part, however, the references have come from different professional journals and books representing single perspectives. The attempt in this book is to respond to identity from a *psychotheological* point of view. By this view I mean a reflection that considers medicine, psychology, social work, and theology. As a psychologist, all of these disciplines are important to me; as a Christian priest, all of these disciplines are offering me the opportunity to grow to be a fully human, consistently free, individual. It is in a corporate reflection, however minimal, that

new thought can be presented which will take into
account the old, but, hopefully, be deeper and wider.

In this book too I want briefly to examine the identity
crisis in more detail. First, I shall examine some psychological attempts to define what we mean by "personal
identity." Second, I shall try to discover how the social
context of the individual affects his identity. Third, I
will examine the conflict between forces which promote
and forces which undermine and destroy personal
identity. Fourth, I shall try to see how we can think
psychotheologically about identity and social change,
and what this means for pastoral care and religious
values. Finally, I will view identity in the light of the
affirmation approach, and herein we will begin the
answer to the question: "Who controls me?"

My total thank-you list is too long to be published.
I shall try, though, to point out major areas of indebted-
ness. My tutor, R. A. Lambourne, M.D., of Great Britain,
has had considerable influence upon my reflections.
Gabriel Marcel of Paris, shortly before his death, en-
couraged me to gather my thoughts and put them in
writing. Anna A. Terruwe, M.D., famed as the dis-
coverer of new psychiatric syndromes as well as dis-
coverer of the approach of Affirmation, has stimulated
my thought in conversation with her in her native city
of Nijmegen in the Netherlands. To my American colleagues, Sister Anna Polcino, M.D., and Conrad W.
Baars, M.D., I am particularly indebted; their sharing
with me in the founding of an international educational
and therapeutic center for religious professionals in

Whitinsville, Massachusetts, has been a daily source of challenge—indeed, a celebration of life. My fear is that some of their material, which got into my head from their lectures and our discussions, might have found its way into the text of this book without appropriate references, as I assimilated in my own practice and thinking what they were sharing with me. Let this then be a reference as well as my expression of appreciation.

In addition to the assistance from professional colleagues, I must also acknowledge two lovely women. I am particularly blessed in having a competent nurse-assistant, Mrs. Ghislaine P. Parenteau, R.N., D.Theo., and a good-spirited secretary, Mrs. Ann K. Ashe; they not only typed (and retyped) the manuscript, but have proofread the copy several times. There must be a special place in heaven for such people.

Finally, I continue to remember with affection the staff and residents of the House of Affirmation, International Therapeutic Center for Clergy and Religious. Especially I am grateful to those persons who allowed me to participate with them in their struggles in times of stress, anxiety, and pain. These relationships have developed into continuing friendships of great meaning.

THOMAS A. KANE

Chapter I

WHO CONTROLS ME?

Who controls me? Who controls my being me?

These are the fundamental questions being asked by men and women throughout the world today. These questions point to a twofold uncertainty. We—men and women—are uncertain who we are as individuals, but we are becoming even more and more uncertain of our identity as communities, as groups, as nations, as neighborhoods, as families.

There has never been an age of man that was not a time of social change. Man has been constantly reordering his social relationships. The rise and expansion of one nation, the decline of another, the spread of the great religions, plagues and famines, new techniques of manufacture, and the vicissitudes of trade have produced new social relationships, new power groupings, new ruling classes, new expert elites, new slaves, and new rejects. As these developments changed societies and nations, they also changed individuals. For example, the changes in Europe that took place during the sixteenth and seventeenth centuries connected with the Reformation and Renaissance had much to do with the aftermath of the black death, the discovery of the New World, and the development of capitalism. But they also came about because individuals were developing new understandings of themselves, new identities. Because of advances in science, geography, economics, men acquired new confidence in their own ability to cope with life. Instead of being inhibited by the fear of imminent death and judgment, they began to value this life as something to be enjoyed and made beautiful, or to be bought and sold. So the Renaissance gentleman, explorer, poet, businessman was a different person from the medieval knight whose hope was to appease divine wrath by endowing the local monastery.

So we see an interaction between personal identity and social change. We should expect to find this today and we do. But today we also find factors which are producing a crisis of identity for the individual and for society. Changes today are happening much faster than before. Advances in technology mean that a man may have to relearn work skills two or three times in his lifetime, or become superfluous. Rural societies are being faced with rapid industrialization and urbanization, with consequent changes in patterns of life and family. The world has become smaller. Social change takes place on a world scale. But this means that the changes taking place in any one society will be affected by what is happening outside that society and, more important, beyond the control of that society.

Radio and television bring instant communication of ideas from one part of the world to another. Increased education means increased awareness. In earlier times change was slow enough to be digested gradually; it is now taking place so rapidly that we are having to learn to live in a continuous state of change. But this makes it more difficult for the individual to work out in which direction he wants to go. It makes it even more difficult for him to feel that he is really in control of what is happening to him or even to know who he is and what his place is in the scheme of things. In medieval times a man might have hated his lord or king, but he at least knew who they were and what they were and, consequently, who he was in relation to them. Today a man is faced with the choice of two apparently opposed political parties that in fact carry out more or less similar policies but that still seem unable to solve society's problems.

Who does control me? Is anyone in control at all? Is the whole world some great machine racing to destruction which cannot be controlled? Who, then, am I, and where am I going? Am I he who has no influence on the course of events? an unheard voice? nothing?

The conditions of change today seem to be producing a crisis of identity. The expression "crisis of identity" is used in connection with a variety of phenomena: with increases in crime and disorderly behavior among young people; with nervous breakdowns among students; with the social problems of minority groups; with the tendency of clergy to look for "secular employ-

ment"; with the unease of voters in their relationship to
elected officials. But the identity crisis means more than
just fundamental uncertainty. The social change responsible causes conflict between power groups and interests. Revolutions and revolutionary movements are concerned with much more than the reordering of the power
structure. They are concerned with the nature of man
himself, and arise from fundamental beliefs as to who
man is. Capitalist, Socialist, Fascist, nationalist, military
ruler—all ultimately have fundamental beliefs about
man, and these are expressed in what their movements
do to the people they control. There are few societies
today in which one such view of man is not being chal-
lenged by another which claims to be fundamentally
opposed to the first. The individual then is faced with
a choice—not just between rulers and types of social
order, but between understandings of himself. Many
persons will face the possibility of a new identity by
clinging more fiercely to the old.

If man can be offered a new identity, if indeed he
can take it upon himself to decide who or what he is
and where he is going, if his identity is made up of
something more than the sum of the psychological,
social, and economic forces acting upon him, this may
imply that he has a true identity and a false identity;
that in some social orders, relationships, work situations
he is more truly himself than in others; and that his
identity may have something to do with his destiny.
If this is so, we are moving into the field of psychotheology. God made man in his own image. We believe
Jesus to be the Word made flesh, Son of man, Man for

others. As such, he judges our efforts to attain true humanity and calls us to find our identity through him. The doctrine of Jesus as the true God become true man will be central in the Church's proclamation. What does this mean for persons with religious values, for the individual Christian? What does it mean for the Church?

Chapter II

IDENTITY AND THE INDIVIDUAL

At first sight it is easy to define identity. If we put together a person's physical appearance, his voice, his habits, his interests, his family and friends, his work and play, his home and possessions, we think we know who he is and what he is. With most people, however, we do not get the opportunity to see all the many facets of personality. If we encounter a person in his work, we may come to different conclusions about him than if we knew him primarily through his hobbies or his son, wife, or parent. The different assessments may be due to more than the fact that he is seen from different standpoints. They may be due to the fact that the individual consciously or unconsciously feels that he is a different person in different situations. He may be efficient or effective at work but disorganized and chaotic at home. He may be a dominating figure at his parish, but docile and obedient at work.

If we develop a close relationship with someone, we may discover that his public identities bear little relation to the person himself. His own self-understanding may not correspond to any of them. He may see himself as someone quite different, who has yet to be revealed. Alternatively, he may be content to let the rest of the world define him as they will. Most likely, he will be uncomfortably aware that none of the identities conferred upon him by others quite corresponds to what he, deep down, believes himself to be. He may be haunted by the fear that his true identity will never be revealed, and that he and the world may never understand who he really is. He wants to do certain things, be certain things, say certain things, love certain people and be loved by them. In short, the individual believes he has a unique contribution to make to the world and believes he cannot be truly himself until he is able to make it.

Identity is something that the individual is not really aware of until he is threatened with its loss. The person who feels he is making his unique contribution to the world will be happy to relate the identities perceived by the world to his essential self. He will feel in control of his image. However, the person who is suffering an identity crisis will feel that he is, in fact, losing control of who he is and that the world is taking over. Alternatively, he may retreat into fantasy in which he makes his own world—one which he can mold and dominate but which cuts him off from the real world.

The achievement of a sense of personal identity is related to the establishment of a satisfactory relationship between the inner self and the outside world. Personal identity is rooted first of all in the struggle to survive—to keep the world sufficiently at bay for basic existence to continue. When this is foremost, other people will be seen as threatening and are to be dominated or to be held off. When the individual is assured of his personal survival, he will need to relate himself to others and establish a group identity. This need is also related to the need to survive, but the individual finds that he can achieve a satisfactory sense of identity only in relation to others. When this has been achieved, he will begin to find that his identity is threatened by the group, and he will want to stand apart from it, defining himself not by the group but by abstract ideals and entering only into those relationships he freely chooses. When his freedom of identity has been achieved, he becomes a contributor to the group.

The contemporary psychologists Jean Piaget and Erik Erikson both see the growth of the individual in terms of the establishment of a mature relationship with the world. Piaget realized that the child developed mental abilities through a dynamic interaction between himself and his environment. Piaget saw mental development as the continuing construction, stage by stage, of a vast building, with each stage being dependent on the completion of the previous stage and able to find its place only in the context of the previous stage. When Piaget speaks of mental development, he means the ability to know and master the environment, not simply passive understanding of it.

The child experiences the world first of all as something to be sucked, then to be pulled, then to be grasped. He assimilates each understanding into himself. This changes his understanding of himself, and he must adapt himself to his new identity, which is then able to master a further new experience. First the child masters his own basic functions of movement, of self-control and sound. He then begins to discover that he is not, as he thought, part of his mother, but that he is separate and he must thus learn to relate to other separate "selfs." So he learns to communicate through language and begins to understand the relationships between people and things. He then learns social behavior. He is not merely one who is separate; rather, he is one who is separate but who relates. At first, social rules and customs are themselves concrete entities into which he must fit. Finally, the young person can begin to grasp abstract concepts. He is now one who can analyze and choose. But this is not the end of the story.

Piaget points out that the interaction continues giving a deeper grasp and understanding of the world and so a firmer sense of himself. For Piaget, true personal identity is a continuing and deepening search, and he who ceases to search loses his identity. Piaget is concerned with the conceptual development of children. It is clear that if the conditions for the construction of his building are missing, and if one of the stages is missed out, the whole can be dislocated. If the child lacks a mother figure to identify with, if he lacks the company of his peers to socialize with, his developmental process may be disrupted, and this may affect his confidence in himself later on. But Piaget is describing process. Given suitably stable conditions, there is no reason why a mature person should not develop.

However, it is clear that this does not always happen. Some persons coming from a highly encouraging environment never seem to develop a sufficient sense of identity to continue to seek and discover themselves and the world. Others coming from situations where everything seems to be against them triumph over adversity. But the necessity to struggle and the effort needed to win makes their sense of identity stronger. People who see life as adventure, as something to be explored and encountered, or who deal creatively with the crises which life brings, seem to develop greater individuality and distinctiveness. They have more confidence in themselves because, as they triumph over each new trial, they become more confident that their basic identity cannot be swamped.

It would seem, then, that when the developmental stages of childhood are complete, there comes a point where the person must take over the machine—where the choosing-and-responding "me" takes over the functioning "me." Erikson pointed to adolescence as the time when this happens or does not happen. Adolescence for Erikson is seen as a period of moratorium, when the major developmental tasks are complete and the person begins to find his place in the world and the direction in which he intends to go. He is looking for a faith to live by, and an effective way of working out that faith. He looks for identity by identification with a number of peer groups, ideologies, ways of behavior, members of the opposite sex. But the basic "I" within gradually develops by reacting in different ways to these various identifications until the young person no longer has to shelter under the identity of others but can become autonomous over his own life and decide in which direction he wishes to move. However, the individual's new sense of autonomy can be preserved only if he can develop long-range goals toward which to move. If he can do this and concentrate his energies on them, his sense of identity will be greatly enhanced, contributing to a deepening of his health and personality. Memory and intelligence and the acquisition of skills and knowledge are greatly improved when the individual can direct his energies to a task connected to long-range goals which he has personally chosen and which are, therefore, an expression of his identity. As he moves toward his goals, he feels less threatened by the world and becomes more confident of his ability to contribute to it and respond to it.

Many people do not achieve this initial autonomy. This can be because it is physically impossible for them to establish long-range goals. Work is all important to the development of a sense of personal identity. If the individual is able to find only work which is dull and repetitive and which demands nothing of him, his desire to contribute to the world will be undermined, and he will feel increasingly unsure of his identity. In order to stifle his doubts, he may cease to develop and cease to ask questions. As we shall see, this can have serious implications for the health of mankind as a whole.

Essential to a sense of personal identity is confidence in relationships with others and the feeling that one is accepted. This develops from early childhood, from trust and confidence in parents, particularly mother. In a survey of some twenty young inmates in a Boston prison, the one thing that was common to all their backgrounds was a failure of parental relationship. In some cases this was a basic lack of love and trust; in others, the breakup of the home, or the death of a parent and subsequent arrival of a stepmother or stepfather.

If the individual is not trusted and accepted, he will not trust and accept himself. He will then accept uncritically the behavior of the peer group and will have no confidence in his own ability to evaluate it. He will never get beyond identification to the discovery of identity and the achievement of autonomy. Much juvenile delinquency seems to come from the need of groups of adolescents who lack this basic confidence in themselves to assert themselves against a society which has refused to accept them.

There are many people who fail to achieve a satisfactory sense of personal identity for no apparent reason that marks them out from those who do. They make a choice to play safe and bury their talents in the soil.

Chapter III

PERSONAL IDENTITY
AND GROUP IDENTITY

If an individual is asked who he is, he will almost certainly reply with reference to one or more group: "I am Nancy Johnson from Boston, daughter of Bill Smith, wife of Bob Johnson. I go to St. Paul's Church and I work at the Second National Bank in Cambridge."

Man is a social being, and individuals define themselves with reference to the groups, families, churches, nations of which they are part. In fact, knowledge of self as part of a larger entity comes before knowledge of self as an individual. The child first becomes aware of himself as part of his mother and later as part of the family group. Both mother and family remain part of the individual throughout his life, and his own sense of identity will depend on how far he succeeds in breaking the dependence of childhood. However, as the child grows and develops, he will wish to function more and more independently of the family. He will do this by finding other groups to identify with. The peer group is all important to the child and particularly to the adolescent, because it allows him to separate himself from the family while at the same time giving him another group or groups with which to identify. The peer group is like the family in that it provides an identity, ready made, with which the young person chooses to identify. Yet peer groups are usually rejected after a short time, as the individual realizes that his own identity is something other than that of the group. He will then often seek another peer group which gives him another experimental identity, but as he becomes more sure of himself as a distinct individual, he will reject the peer group altogether. He will now join groups which freely associate around some goal or activity but which lack the compulsive identification of the peer group.

The mature adult will express and develop his identity by joining a number of groups to express different aspects of himself. He will join, for example, particular sports clubs, political parties, fraternities or other interest groups, because they represent people to whom he can give and from whom he can receive something of himself. As the individual becomes more confident of his own identity, groups become less important, and he will tend to rely more on relationships in depth with a few close friends. He will still participate in groups but will not depend on them.

We have seen that where an individual has failed to develop initial self-confidence in himself, he is likely to identify totally with a group or indeed with his family and be unable to think of himself apart from them. This reveals a basic lack of confidence in his own accept-ability, as he believes that if he acts independently of the group, the group will disown him. When the group for any reason collapses or declines, he is likely to suffer extreme anxiety.

We have been discussing the role of the group in relation to the development of the individual's sense of identity. Groups, however, have an identity of their own which is more than the sum of the individuals composing them. Every individual shares the identity of the groups to which he belongs, and their identity is part of his. The obvious examples are racial and national. Other examples are religion, family, supporters of baseball teams, clubs, and school. These identities are fundamen-tally related to the need for survival. They are related to the instinct that there is a particular territory, or be-lief, or way of life, or means of self-assertion or support which must be defended and into which we can retreat. Those who are with us behind the stockade, whether it be a physical stockade enclosing a particular patch of land or a more nebulous stockade enclosing people of a particular creed or outlook, are with us and part of us. Those outside may be against us, seeking to take over and stop us being us. This instinct for group survival is so fundamental that it persists long after it has ceased to correspond to any reality. For example, notice how cer-tain immigrant groups in America have maintained their identity long after there is any need to group together for survival.

The group identity represents two other needs for personal identity: the need of the individual to know where he stands in space and in time. It is important for an individual to know that there is a particular community in a particular place to which he belongs and which gives him a place. It also enables him to distinguish himself from the rest of mankind. Compatriots abroad will gather together on their national day and do things they would be doing at home even though during the rest of the year they will mix quite happily with the "natives." For some people, associations based on the old school or college or common experiences in a youth organization retain a strong pull. People return to visit their native towns long after they have left them or return year after year to the same vacation spots. People who own their homes take much greater part in community life than those who do not. A sense of place gives a sense of belonging, a feeling that here acceptability is assured while elsewhere it may have to be fought for. On the other hand, the familiar community very often accepts only on its own terms, and many people find that they can only fully express their identity by leaving. But the relationship remains and the desire to return never dies.

Even more important than a sense of place is the need for a sense of history. A group identity often represents a shared past which extends back many generations. "A wandering Armenian was my father—and he went down into Egypt and sojourned there, few in number: and there he became a nation, great, mighty and populous. And the Egyptian afflicted us . . . and the Lord brought us out of Egypt with a mighty hand and an outstretched arm, with great terror, with signs and wonders; and he brought us into this place and gave us this land, a land flowing with milk and honey." (Deut. 25:5-6; 8-9)

This was how the Jews of later generations described themselves and still describe themselves. Their identity as a people depended on certain past events which had particular significance. These events defined their uniqueness and their relationship with other people. They had a right to exist as a people, a right to be themselves. Their identity is authenticated by their history. Their history belongs to each individual Jew, and nothing can take it from him. The history symbolizes also the common values of the nation. It authenticates law and ritual, and the upholding of these values is an important aspect of identity. The Jews are perhaps the group which has clung most fiercely to their identity despite the most adverse circumstances.

But all national groups have a past, usually idealized, which serves to authenticate their identity and distinctiveness. Our American identity, for example, is founded on the fact that the early immigrants fled from tyranny to seek freedom and create a just society; the emphasis on individual freedom is very much part of what it is to be American. The Jewish and American identities represent a standing for certain values and ideals, defending them against attack, where necessary.

Group identity is a necessary part of human identity. It is something everyone has and everyone needs. It is clear, however, that it can be either a constructive or destructive influence. Those who are most confident of the traditions and identity of their own group tend to be those who will be most open to establish relationships with other groups. They will be interested in establishing points of contact and common factors and be anxious to discover and celebrate a common humanity across barriers. They find that their own identity is deepened and enhanced in discovering members of other groups and nationalities. For example, we find that in the ecumenical movement, it is those who are confident in their own faith through the life of their own denominations who are prepared to reach out to discover something still greater in the wider church. Group identity then provides a healthy foundation for the personal-identity search of the individual.

Group identity can be destructive where the individual is unable to see himself apart from it. As we have seen, group identity is an important aspect of personal identity. It enables the individual to define who he is in relation to others, and gives him location in time and space. Erikson[1] maintains that a true personal identity depends upon the support the individual receives from the collective sense of identity of the social groups which are significant to him. This support should give him the confidence to be open to the future, to accept that his own identity and that of the groups in which he participates is incomplete, and to have the courage to allow both his individual and group identities to change and develop—or, indeed, to face the more threatening possi-

---

[1]Erik Erikson, "Identity and Uprootedness in Our Time," in *Insight and Responsibility* (New York: W. W. Norton & Company, 1964).

bility of death and resurrection. Where, however, the group identity is threatened, he may resort to what Erikson calls the "total mode of identifying himself and relating to the world." Totality for Erikson means that an absolute boundary is placed around those things which the individual can see and of which he can be convinced. New experiences are either fitted into the closed system or rejected as not being part of reality. When the identity of a group is threatened, either from domination by a stronger group or because the group members are unable to adapt to a changing world, the members of that group will adopt a totalitarian identity in self-defense. This is a feature of adolescent peer groups, and, as we have seen, it is emphasized where adolescents have not received adequate support from the family.

In society, generally, total group identity manifests itself in two ways: in prejudice and in ideology. Prejudice is part of the natural defense mechanism of a group against other groups. When a group feels that its identity is threatened, it will tend to project its anxiety onto another group, usually—and in particular—onto the characteristics of this group which threatens it.

Ideology comes from a threat to individual rather than group identity. Ideology, like prejudice, implies a closed view of reality. Ideology is not necessarily destructive. In certain circumstances it can give the individual strength to survive extreme situations. It also gives individuals conviction in the face of persecution or adversity that their being cannot be ultimately destroyed. It was the people with internalized religious values who showed the most resilience in concentration camps in World War II. In normal times, however, ideological groups are a means for individuals to preserve their identity without having to expose it to the challenge of the real world. Typical examples in the Western world are groups identified with ultraconservative religious groups and with Marxism. Marxism is essentially a method of evaluating particular aspects of reality—the relationships between economic forces and social structures. Some people, however, identify themselves totally with one way of looking at things and identify only one aspect of reality with the whole. By becoming a group which focuses on an ideology, the individual assumes the identity of the group. This prevents him from encountering reality and cuts off the dialogue between self and the world which leads to the discovery of personal identity.

Chapter IV

PERSONAL IDENTITY
AND SOCIAL CHANGE

So far, in speaking of man and the world, we have spoken in terms of man and society. We have seen that personal identity depends on the individual establishing a dialectical relationship with society which enables him to identify with it yet stand apart from it. Social change and revolution appear, then, to be the establishment of those social relationships in which the individual can best pursue his identity. However, social change is primarily about man's relationship to the created order and, above all, about the sharing of the fruits of the earth. In the first two chapters of Genesis we read: "And God blessed them [man and woman] and said to them, Be fruitful and multiply. Fill the earth and subdue it; and have dominion over the fish of the sea and over the birds of the air and over every living thing." Later we read: ". . . The Lord God formed every beast of the field . . . and brought them to man to see

43

what he would call them: whatever man called every living creature, that was its name." (Gen. 1:28; 2:19)

Man is to subdue the earth and have dominion over it; but he is also given the task of carrying on the work of the Creator in his relationship with the world. In naming it, man gives the created order its identity and defines it in relation to himself. But the created order gives man his earthly task. Through his relationship with the created order, man discovers what he is for. He knows who he is by his work upon the created order. He grows crops, he rears cattle, he makes things out of wood and metal. He subdues the earth, but he also contributes to it. He finds and expresses his identity by bringing order and beauty.

For the writer of Genesis, however, this was no arbitrary relationship. Man is the agent of God in the world to order both the created order and his own social and political relationships in accordance with the laws of his being which God has ordained. What Genesis is saying is the fundamental truth; that right relationship with God consists not just in right social relationships but that these must be rooted in a creative dialectical relationship with the created order.

Chapter V

OPPRESSION AND LOSS OF IDENTITY

If we examine the pressures and social change and revolution in the world today, we will find that they can be traced to a protest at the breaking of man's relationship with the created order and the desire to restore it. Most, if not all, the revolutionary movements are about the sharing of the fruits of the earth, and aim to overthrow those political systems which enable one group to exploit the resources at the expense of the whole people. But exploitation and oppression affect people's evaluation of themselves, so the throwing off of oppression involves the discovery of a new identity. Where it does not, the postrevolutionary social order soon begins to show many of the features of the regime it has overthrown. Soviet Russia, for example, has continued many of the oppressive features of czarist rule, such as an omnipresent secret police and a ruthless autocratic government. The Russians have failed to realize that altering institutional structures is insufficient if the people involved in those structures have not in the revolution gained a new understanding of themselves and society.

Oppression distorts not only the relationship of people to one another but also their relationship to the created order. When people are being used as tools, they are unable to form their own relationships with the created order and so are unable to seek their own identity. They are forced to accept the spurious slave identity which the oppressor conveys upon them. Referring to the situation of the American Negro, the black leader Stokely Carmichael says:

> Thus, black people came to be depicted as "lazy," "apathetic," "dumb," "shiftless," "good-timers." Just as red men had to be recorded as "savages" to justify the white men's theft of their land, so the black men had to be vilified in order to justify their continued oppression. Those who have the right to define are masters of the situation.[2]

In the same way, the oppressor distorts his own relationship with the created order, seeing it only in terms of exploitation. For him, his fellowmen become the means of this exploitation. He is trapped in a false understanding of the world and so of his own being. James Baldwin, addressing his fellow black Americans, writes, concerning white people:

> They are, in effect, still trapped in a history which they do not understand; until they understand it they cannot be re-

---

[2]Stokely Carmichael & Charles V. Hamilton, *Black Power: The Policies of Liberation in America* (New York: Random House, 1968).

leased from it. They have had to believe for many years that black men are inferior to white men. Many indeed know better, but, as you will discover, people find it difficult to act on what they know. To act is to be committed and to be committed is to be in danger. In this case the danger in the minds of most white Americans is the loss of their identity. . . . If the word "integration" means anything, this is what it means: that we, with love, shall force our brothers to see themselves as they are, to cease fleeing from reality and begin to change it . . .[3]

---

[3]James Baldwin, *The Fire Next Time* (New York: Dial Press, 1963).

Chapter VI

TECHNOLOGY AND FALSE IDENTITY

The loss of identity of both oppressor and oppressed runs much deeper than the simple fact of colonial and racial oppression. What seems to be happening is that man's relationship with the created order has become unbalanced. Man is putting all his energies into subduing the earth rather than contributing to it and opening himself to it. The most important development in man's relationship to the created order has been the growth of scientific knowledge and its application in technology. Technology, as Harvey Cox has pointed out, is liberating. It ends man's bondage to the earth and enables him to enjoy it. It provides greater possibilities for expressing his relationship to the created order and so for gaining a fuller knowledge of himself.

But technology has its dangers. In the first place, mass production in industry means that the individual worker is unable to make his own creative contribution to the manufacturing process. He becomes a cog in the machine. Instead of the machine being the means of extending man's domination over the earth, the man becomes an extension of the machine. This affects his estimate of himself. He is, in effect, a slave of the machine, and must either accept the identity of a slave or feel alienated from his own work. Consequently, he begins to doubt his own identity. Gabriel Marcel, a contemporary French philosopher, offers a concrete illustration.

> Traveling on the subway, I often wonder with a kind of dread what can be the inward reality of the life of this or that man employed on the railway—the man who opens the doors, for instance, or the one who punches the tickets. Surely everything both within him and outside him conspires to identify this man with his functions—meaning not only with his functions as worker, as trade union member or as a voter, but with his vital functions as well. The rather horrible expression "time table" perfectly describes his life. So many hours for each function. Sleep too is a function which must be discharged so that the other functions may be exercised in their turn. The same with pleasure, with relaxation; it is logical that the weekly allowance of recreation should be determined by an expert on hygiene; recreation is a psycho-organic function which must not be neglected any more than, for instance, the function of sex. We need go no further; this sketch is sufficient to suggest the emergence of a kind of vital schedule; the details will vary with the country, the climate, the profession, etc., but what matters is that there is a schedule.[4]

Mass production often creates two classes in society;

---

[4]Gabriel Marcel, *The Philosophy of Existentialism* (New York: Citadel Press, 1956).

those who own the means of production and exchange and those who actually operate and work them. Like the white Americans described by James Baldwin, the owner class frequently becomes trapped. Its members find themselves using the machine and their employees to subdue the earth but not to contribute to it. So their relationship to the created order is unbalanced and their search for their identity is compromised. The result of all this is that instead of the machine liberating man, man becomes the slave of the machine. In fact, society is modeling itself on the machine.

Mass production created mass society. In mass society, the individual is not expected to seek a unique identity of his own but is expected to conform to society's norm and fit in with the overall pattern. Thus, as we have seen, in the mass society, the individual is a cog rather than a contributor in his work. He is expected to buy what the advertiser directs, live where the zoning board permits, wear what fashion dictates, go on package vacations. The pressure is on the individual to play a predetermined role rather than to work out his personal identity. Where the personal identity emphasizes the individual's uniqueness, the role emphasizes his conformity, his ability to fit in. He will not search and explore in order to understand more deeply the world and himself because his place in the world is clearly defined. All he has to do is fit in. When he vacations abroad, for example, he expects the airport, the hotel, the diet, etc., to conform to what he already knows. Differences are "quaint" and even "interesting," at a safe distance, but to encounter them is profoundly disturbing. So the individual eventually loses the ability to assimilate and adapt to new experiences. His identity ceases to grow. He is frozen in the consumer role. Charles Reich, in his penetrating study *The Greening of America,* illustrates the alienating effect of mass consumer society by painting a picture of a "young attractive couple," both college educated—he with a profession or executive position in some organization—with a home and several children. Their house is attractively furnished: they have antiques, books, original prints. They enjoy entertaining; they read a lot. They love the out-of-doors; they ski in winter, sail in summer. They enjoy good music, plays, and art. They spend time with their children and "travel to some off-beat place each year." What, asks Reich, is wrong with this picture?

> How, then, have we the right to suggest that with our young couple, all of their living is false? Marx and Marcuse distinguish between those needs which are a product of a person's authentic self and those which are imposed from outside by society. Why does an individual ski? Is it based on self-knowledge or lack of self-knowledge—on advertising and other pressures from society? If the latter, it will not really satisfy the self or enable the self to grow. . . . All the young couple's activities have the quality of separateness from self, of fitting some pattern—a pattern already known and only waiting to be fulfilled.[5]

Reich concludes that this kind of consciousness is convinced that man's needs are best met by dominating

---

[5]Charles Reich, *The Greening of America: How the Youth Revolution Is Trying to Make America Liveable* (New York: Random House, 1970).

experience rather than being subject to it. In his relationship with the world, man is only interested in what he can control. He "is the victim of a cruel deception. He has been persuaded that the richness of life is to be found in power, success, popularity, and achievement." He "wants nothing to do with dread, awe, mystery, accidents, failure, helplessness, magic. He has been deprived of the search for self that makes only these experiences possible."[6]

The dominant institution in Western society is the international corporation which is the controlling model for mass society. Often, the corporation represents power without responsibility. Many times, it represents the organization of man to fit the machine and is devoted not to the liberation of men to discover themselves but to greater and more efficient mass production. To achieve this, it needs depersonalized men and women who will, on the one hand, serve it without question and, on the other hand, consume its products—also without question. The corporations are able, therefore, to determine the life styles of whole societies. By their complete control of the means of production—on what shall be produced and who shall produce it—the corporations can control what men eat; where, how, and increasingly, if they work; and what kind of lives they lead. They raise sharply the question "Who controls me and who controls my being me?" because, being international, the corporations are responsible to no one, yet they can and do wield great power in international and internal politics.

---

[6]Ibid.

The American Watergate experience is a good example of vested interests. The individual is increasingly aware that his elected representatives—his communal self—are ultimately powerless against the international business community. Left-wing groups personalize international capitalism and compile dossiers on the interests of those they reckon to be key individuals in international organizations. This is rather like shooting peas at a tank. For, to quote Charles Reich again on the power structure of the corporation:

> From all this there emerges the great revelation about the executive suite—the place from which power hungry men seem to rule society. In the executive suite, there may be a Leger or Braque on the wall. There may be a vast glass and metal desk. But there is no one there. No one at all is in the executive suite. What looks like a man is only a representation of a man who does what the organization requires. He does not run the machine, he *tends* it.[7]

Man is subject to a faceless machine which forces him into a predetermined mold. Those who recognize this and reject the mass society are themselves rejected and seen as criminals to be punished. They are patients to be cured, social problems to be solved, children to be "schooled." Technological society never raises the question whether society's answer is appropriate to the individual. The end result of all this would seem to be a loss of nerve on the part of technological society. Despite its domination of the physical world, it is unable

---

[7]Ibid.

to solve its human problems. Men look into the past to find out if not who they are, at least who they were. Meanwhile, communal and racial jealousy increase, city centers decay, and the gap between rich and poor, developed and underdeveloped, widens. It is often said that man has the technical know-how to solve these problems, if only he had the will. In fact, it is not strictly true that man "has" the technical know-how. He may have the knowledge but he is very far from controlling it. To solve these problems implies a further stage in man's voyage of discovery of himself and the world. Such voyages of discovery, however, cannot be permitted. They might stop the machine.

Chapter VII

REVOLUTION AND THE RECOVERY OF IDENTITY

Revolution is dangerous. As we have seen from the example of the Soviet Union, it can amount to little more than a rearrangement of the power structure. It can lead to changes in the goals and attitudes of society only if people's understanding of themselves changes. Paulo Freire defines revolution as a vocation to humanization. Freire sees man as "an uncompleted being conscious of his incompletion. . . . In order for the struggle against oppression to have meaning, the oppressed must not become the oppressors of the oppressors but the restorers of humanity to all."[8]

Freire points out that the struggle for freedom is dangerous because it opens up for the person the fact of his incompleteness. The individual only becomes in-

---

[8]Paulo Freire, *Pedagogy of the Oppressed* (New York: Herder & Herder, 1968).

volved in the struggle at the point at which he realizes
that he is not truly himself and cannot discover himself
within the existing order. The struggle, at whatever
level, opens up the unknown at the heart of the person
and uncovers possibilities of both humanization and de-
humanization.

In the thought of Freire, Frantz Fanon and others,
we find a rediscovery of the dialectical relationship between man and the world. As man sets about changing
the world, he himself is changed. As the true nature of
the world and his situation in it are unveiled to him,
he becomes determined to change these so as to restore
his identity. The oppressed need to break away from the
identity imposed upon them by the oppressor.

> The oppressed, having internalized the image of the op-
> pressor and adopted his guidelines, are fearful of freedom.
> Freedom would require them to eject this image and re-
> place it with autonomy and with responsibility. . . . Freedom
> is not an ideal located outside of man. . . . It is rather the in-
> dispensable condition for the quest of human identity.[9]

Frantz Fanon in *A Dying Colonialism* gives some
interesting examples of the changes of consciousness
which he sees taking place because of the Algerian independence struggle. One example concerns the wear-
ing of the veil by Algerian women. Traditionally, the
veil symbolizes the bondage of the Algerian women and
the rigidity of Algerian society. The woman's place in
society, her relationship to men—and so her identity—

---

[9]Ibid.

were determined by society. The veil was also the symbol of Algerian distinctiveness and cultural resistance to French influence. The French, therefore, saw women as the key to cultural penetration of Algerian society— the undermining of Algerian identity leading to total cultural integration with France. They directed educational and propaganda pressure toward unveiling the women, whose situation they regarded as barbaric and medieval. So the veil became the symbol of Algerian resistance. During the war of independence in Algeria, women gradually became drawn into the fighting. This meant the rejection of the veil by the women fighters, as they needed to be independent and highly mobile. This had two results. In the first place, the women fighters had to come to terms with a new relation to the world, which implied a new identity.

> Without the veil she has the impression of her body being cut up into bits; the limbs seem to lengthen indefinitely. She has the impression of being improperly dressed, even naked. . . . The Algerian woman who walks stark naked into the European city relearns her body, reestablishes it in a totally new fashion. The new dialectic of the woman and the world is primary in the case of one revolutionary woman.[10]

Secondly, her relationship with the male world changed. Now that she had made an independent decision to join the revolution, she broke the stylized hierarchical family relationship. Fathers, husbands, brothers

---

[10]Frantz Fanon, *A Dying Colonialism,* trans. Haakon Chevalier (New York: Grove Press, 1970).

had to rediscover the woman as a person. The revolutionary "sister" replaced the veiled chattel. At a later date, the women reassumed the veil, but their choice was a free decision because it can be used to conceal compromising articles about the person. Before, only a few women were involved in the war. Later, all women, veiled and unveiled, came under suspicion, so all were involved. "This was the time during which men, women, children, the whole Algerian people experienced at one and the same time their national vocation and the recasting of the new Algerian society."[11]

This is one way in which a people discovers a new identity in a revolutionary struggle. In a situation such as that in Algeria, the struggle is over clear-cut issues. In Western industrial society the situation is much more complex, and the assault on the personal identity of the individual much more subtle. Charles Reich, Paulo Freire, and Ivan Illich identify the education system as one of the principal battlegrounds. For Reich, the school is where the child learns to play a role, where he is trained to obey rather than to think, for hierarchy rather than democracy. School is ". . . a prison with the ability to an aim . . . an all-out assault on the emerging adolescent self."[12]

Ivan Illich sees the school system as comparable with the medieval initiation by stages into the mysteries of alchemy—the blazing of a false trail to a spurious

---

[11]Freire, op. cit.
[12]Reich, op. cit.

identity.[13] Freire criticizes what he calls the "banking" concept of education, when students are treated as receptacles. In my view, Freire reaches the heart of the matter when he asserts that the "banking" concept assumes a dichotomy between man and the world in which man is seen as spectator rather than a creator. "Banking" education regulates the way in which the world enters into students rather than enabling them to encounter it. Education, too, is becoming dominated by the machine. The emphasis is more and more on the mastery of techniques rather than the "leading out" of the person. Students expect to be trained in techniques which will enable them to control reality rather than to explore it. Education and social science students are trained to "handle" classes or clients rather than to open their personalities to them. Even theological students want to master techniques of biblical criticism and ethical systems. The current fashion for "religious studies" courses probably reflects this fascination with techniques and systems outside the self. The one thing to avoid is an encounter with the living God either by looking theologically at the world or by a reflection on what is happening to oneself.

For Freire, education which makes men free must be seen as praxis—as the response of the individual to the concrete problems of his own existence. This "problem posing" education is based on the development of

---

[13]Ivan Illich, "The Alternative to Schooling," *Saturday Review,* June 1971.

a critical awareness of the world as it is. This awareness obliges students to respond to the challenge of their situation and struggle to overcome the forces—political, economic, or spiritual—which limit them. Problem-posing education is based on creative action arising from critical reflection on the world. Men, says Freire, become authentic beings when engaged in inquiry and creative transformation of their situation in the world. In other words, education is related to establishing man's relationship with the world and so discovering his true self. Education should consist of inviting people to explore the world and to know themselves in responding to its challenges. This takes us back to Piaget, who discovered that conceptual ability is developed by the person solving immediate problems of existence and then adapting himself to the knowledge of himself thus gained. He changes the world, and as he does so, the world enters his being and changes *it.* In adult life this implies a mode of living in which to live is to discover, to know, and to discover further; to come to a knowledge of myself as he-who-is-becoming.

Revolution means, in Freire's own words, to create conditions in which "knowledge at the level of *Doxa* (praise of God) is replaced by knowledge at the level of *Logos* (the Word among us)."[14]

This can only happen at the level of community, and in fact only begins to happen when communities or groups within communities turn from the narrow goal of greater productivity of material wealth and begin

---

[14]Freire, op. cit.

to look for more human ways of living. As we have seen in the Algerian situation, it is at this point that the individuals begin to discover who they are. And that they have an identity other than that assigned to them by the anonymous economic overlord.

Revolution, then, is about the recovery of man's identity, individually and in community, in the recovery of his relationship with the world. It is a revolving to that which is most natural to man.

Chapter VIII

IDENTITY, SOCIAL CHANGE, AND RELIGIOUS VALUES

In this book I have been making two assumptions which raise psychotheological questions. I have assumed that man discovers his identity only in the context of a right relationship with the created order. But I have also assumed that man is distinct from the created order—that, in terms of Genesis, man discovers his identity not *from* the created order but in carrying out his mission *with* the created order. For the writer of Genesis, man's identity is conferred upon him by God and expressed in his relationship with the created order. Adam and Eve allow themselves to be dominated by the created order (represented by the serpent), with the result that they become alienated from God. They become aware of their nakedness and inadequacy and lose confidence in who they are.

We could no doubt see human history as man pur-
suing false identities, other gods, material wealth, and
technology and being recalled by God, by his actions
in history and by his prophets, to his true self. In carrying out the divine mission, there is always before him
the vision of the recovery of his lost identity. "They will
be my people and I will be their God." (Ezek. 37:27)

We have seen that there are forces which threaten
to destroy man by abolishing his distinctiveness from
the world. It is man's fear that he will be overcome by
these forces. It is man's hope that he will attain freedom
from their power.

In Jesus we see man in perfect relationship with
God, seeking the recovery of man's creative relationship
with the world. The fourth Gospel sees Jesus as LOGOS,
as the principle which unites man and the created order
to the reality behind the universe. For the Gospel writer,
the meaning of the universe is expressed in the life and
death of Jesus the perfect Man. Encountering Jesus on
the cross, the Roman centurion says, "Surely this was
the Son of God." In other words, the moment when it
seemed that Jesus, like the rest of mankind, had been
destroyed by the created order, was the moment when
he revealed the true identity of man in relation to the
reality behind the universe. In fact, Jesus could not be
contained by the world, and so liberated man from the
threat of its domination. Man then is distinct from the
world and cannot be ultimately destroyed by the world.

Today, as we have seen, man is threatened by the
domination of technology and technological values. In
Jesus we can assert that man can refuse to be fitted into

the technological scheme of things. We can assert further that it is part of the mystery of humanity—that it is logically and practically impossible to fit human beings into any framework. The excesses of modern society can and indeed do unleash terrible forces of destruction, but they cannot and will not obliterate man, individually or collectively. It is in the struggle to overcome the forces of evil in asserting his right to work out his identity that he is joined to God in Christ, and so becomes truly himself.

In Christianity man's identity is the key to the fulfillment of the command "Love your neighbor as yourself." (Matt. 22:30) This great commandment cannot be fulfilled unless a person is aware of his own dignity and feelings. However, when we speak of love as the outcome of identity, what are we saying? We are simply saying that because of a fulfilled sense of identity, he can feel or experience how another person feels.

Launching oneself into a genuine relationship with another fails to occur when people are treated as objects or statistics, not as persons. Gabriel Marcel makes this clear.

> Those engaged in humanitarian work have to confront an endless number of "cases"; yet the fact remains that if the other is a "presence," he cannot be a "case," and although he presents a problem which falls into a statistical pattern (e.g. the fifteenth alcoholic admitted to the hospital that day), the sense in which the problem is "he" cannot be dealt with statistically.[15]

---

[15]David E. Roberts, *Existentialism and Religious Belief* (New York: Oxford University Press, 1959).

Another reason many people have trouble treating others as unique persons is because they no longer view others as a mystery. Anna A. Terruwe, the Dutch psychiatrist, Gabriel Marcel, the French philosopher, and Anthony Padovano, the American theologian, all agree man is a mystery and cannot be reduced to a "problem." According to Judeo-Christian tradition, "God created man in His image" (Gen. 1:27), and certainly God is a mystery.

Perhaps the reason God is dead for many people today is because the influence of life-giving warmth and communion of understanding is missing in society, and this relationship must be experienced as a preparation for a dynamic relationship with the living God.

Our society can promote love through social structures which value and promote meaningful relationships. It is not asked that we return to an agrarian society but to help make our bureaucratic society become less alienated and less alienating. The great overemphasis Riesman (especially in his book *The Lonely Crowd*) and others have found placed upon social conformity, noninvolvement, and making persons into things is not surprising, for our educational system usually does not try to promote the kind of learning which is most important; namely, development of self-awareness in regard to our feelings and thoughts, and an understanding of our anxiety in making plans and choices.

The integration of social systems with religious values can result in a better society if social systems will give recognition, security, approval, concern, and understanding. Religious and social systems must work together if the immediacy of love is to be realized, not just as an intellectual abstract religious value, but as a concrete secular reality.

It follows then that the style of people with religious values cannot be proselytization and conquest but service and healing, as illustrated in the considerations of Vatican II. Religious values seek to restore all men to true humanness rather than build up its institutions. The Church then is not a fortress but a "liberated zone," and a sign of what man is meant to be, and a witness and celebration of the fact that in Jesus' death and destruction, physical or spiritual cannot contain him.

The Church then is an enabler and teacher. It does not force people into identity but offers an opportunity to build up a community where people can share a common search, and it challenges those who have settled for false identities. It brings before man that true identity that is found only in actively sharing with other men. Against the disintegrating influence of the dominance of the machine, man asserts the fact that his true nature is corporate. The Church does not seek to draw people out of the world but to seek points of contact with the world and to draw together all those who are in different ways seeking man's true humanity, to enable them to discover the oneness behind their several visions. The Church heals by presenting a vision of unity, truth, and goodness. It restores identity by pointing to the risen Lord as he is experienced and celebrated in the Christian community. This means a political commitment, as the struggle for humanity is a political struggle. It is not the Church's mission to desert Constantine for Che but to challenge both Constantine and Che with the Triumphant reigning from the cross. Man must begin to see temporal concerns and drives as one with his spiritual destiny. Religious values and the changing social milieu have a reciprocal relationship.

Chapter IX

AFFIRMATION AND IDENTITY

Denial, as we have seen in the previous chapters, leads to a false identity. Whether denial is directed toward one individual or group, or toward a social process, it is usually done with the attempt to control. For example, a young child who enters a social system for education, treatment, or any other reason should be accepted despite his errors, praised for his efforts, loved for who he is, and be provided with persons worthy of emulation if he is to internalize the concepts of love of neighbor and God. A young child, like any other individual, does not mature by unnecessary criticism or by another's accentuating the negative in him. One denies the other by constantly reminding him of his errors, his shortcomings, his immaturity, without first having loved the other for who he is. Underdeveloped countries are denied advancement by economically powerful countries that try to control them by imposing on them their own cultural and spiritual values. Scientific progress has not led to man's fulfillment; often it has meant only denial. Many are groping about in our age of "progress" bewildered and made bitter by the trends that deny them, individually or corporately.

The primary source of meaning in life, the primary constituency of true identity, is affirmation. In their penetrating study *Loving and Curing the Neurotic*,[16] two internationally recognized psychiatrists write:

> Whereas authentic affirmation is truly life-giving, denial kills. . . . Authentic affirmation is much more than speaking a word of encouragement or the giving of a compliment. It focuses on the very being of the other, on his goodness as a unique human being. It presupposes openness, confident expectation, and uninterrupted attention to everything that happens in the other, to all he is not able to express, and to all the anticipated good within him, even though the other himself is still unsuspecting of that future good.

Dr. Terruwe has called affirmation the essence and core of all mature love. The most tender, delicate, indeed, healing touch is that I allow the other person to be as he is, immaturity and shortcomings included. I do so not out of fear but out of free choice, and allow the other to be who he is so that his full potential may be realized. Affirmation is precisely what is needed for achieving appreciation of self and true identity in relation to others and the created order. An affirmed person does not suffer from a loss of conscious awareness of his own importance.

Anna Terruwe's approach of affirmation may at first seem difficult to grasp, yet we can easily recognize the reality that the primary source of a person's fulfillment

---

[16]Anna A. Terruwe and Conrad W. Baars, *Loving and Curing the Neurotic* (New Rochelle, N. Y.: Arlington House, 1972).

lies in another person, the so-called "significant other."
"The longing to possess our identity is an irreducible
human longing," the Dutch psychiatrist states.

A scriptural illustration of the meaning of affirmation
is found in the account of the meeting of Jesus with
Zacchaeus, the tax collector. Neither accepted nor loved,
Zacchaeus desires to be accepted by others simply for
being who he is. Such acceptance he had not known,
and he evidently placed some hope in Jesus of Nazareth.
Jesus was to pass through his neighborhood and there
would be a crowd to see him. Like other times, because
of occupation and physical appearance, Zacchaeus would
be denied again. Trying to get a view of Jesus, Zacchaeus—so small in stature—could not work his way
through the crowd. He climbed a fig tree on the side of
the road hoping to view the Nazarene.

Jesus does not pass him by but accepts him as he is.
"Zacchaeus, come down because I must stay with you
today," Jesus calls out to the little man in the tree. What
is the result? Zacchaeus immediately is opened—like a
flower in bloom.

Zacchaeus stood there, and said to the Lord: "Here
and now, I give away half of my possessions to charity,
and if I have cheated anyone, I am ready to repay him
four times over."

Charity and justice, then, are the fruits of the man
who has been affirmed, who has been liberated, as they
are also of the man who has been redeemed by Jesus
Christ.

The idea of affirmation opens new perspectives not
only for individuals but for society as a whole. Contem-

porary human society finds hopeful promise in its quest
for identity and freedom from control; the building of
a healing society depends on this fundamental factor of
identity-affirmation. People with religious values, in particular, should be affirming of their fellowman.

Bernard Jan Alfrink, Cardinal Archbishop of Utrecht,
in a speech in Whitinsville, Massachusetts, stated: "We
find that non-Christian people are often irritated by the
fact that Christianity calls itself the religion of love,
while at the same time it has not succeeded in building
up much of a real *communio* not even in its own circles.
Marxism rebukes Christians for always talking about
God and about love, while forgetting at the same time
to make the world a place worth living in for everyone.
And who would dare to say that Christians could justly
ignore this rebuke without even making the beginning
of an examination of conscience?

"Perhaps the problem could be posited this way, that
the world today is honestly dissatisfied with religion as
it presents itself and rightly asks of religion to be taken
seriously by the Church. Very often the world of today
experiences the religious person as one who is not happy
himself and does not make others happy. To the world
the religious person resembles the famous Prometheus
of Greek mythology. Chained immovably to a rock,
bound, not free, and tortured by an eagle picking at his
liver, he suffered interior pains, division, uncertainty,
dissatisfaction, intolerance. ". . . It could be very interesting and at the same time instructive to see how
often in the Scriptures the word 'joy' is written and used

as a kind of label for the believer—as the eye-catcher of a poster, so to speak, for the Christian. 'I have spoken thus to you, that my joy may be in you, and that your joy may be complete.' In human intercourse it is always

the human being who gives joy and happiness to the other. It is the Christian who should take first place in this art of affirming his fellowman. But he who wants to affirm his fellowman will have to be affirmed himself first by someone else. Only the one who has blossomed out in affirmation is able to open up and affirm the other. It is not difficult to see how so many people are asking to be affirmed by someone else: the man who is lonely for whatever reason, or the man in the midst of an identity crisis who no longer recognizes himself and is uncertain of himself. To affirm and to be affirmed is a matter of fundamental interaction in human society. One who has not been affirmed by others is not able to affirm others. He will soon deny the other in the futile hope of improving his own situation through self-affirmation."

It is evident from what has been said thus far that there is required much more new and bold thinking if we are to meet the challenge of the future. Affirmation can effect the future; it does not, however, seek to control; it is like the sun upon the rose bringing it to blossom.

Having been affirmed by another and affirming others, I will know and feel who I am; I will have a true identity. I will sense that I am different but acceptable, that I belong in the world but that I am contributing to it and can change it; that there is a unique place for me and that I have a unique contribution, that I can choose freely to do and to love, that I cannot be ultimately destroyed and am confidently open to what is to come.

BIBLIOGRAPHY

Baldwin, James. *The Fire Next Time*. New York: Dial Press, 1963.

Carmichael, Stokely S., and Hamilton, Charles V. *Black Power: The Realities of Liberation in America*. New York: Random House, 1968.

Coyle, Alcuin, O.F.M. *Church Under Tension*. New York: Catholic Book Publishers Company, 1972.

Erikson, Erik H. *Insight and Responsibility*. New York: W. W. Norton & Company, 1964.

Fanon, Frantz. *A Dying Colonialism*. Translated by Haakon Chevalier. New York: Grove Press, 1970.

Freire, Paulo. *Pedagogy of the Oppressed*. New York: Herder & Herder, 1968.

Illich, Ivan. "The Alternative to Schooling." *Saturday Review*, June 1971.

Josephson, M. E. *Man Alone: Alienation in Modern Society*. New York: Dell Publishing Co., 1963.

Lambourne, R. A. *Community, Church and Healing*. London: Darton, Longman, Todd, 1963.

Marcel, Gabriel. *En chemin, vers quel eveil?* Paris: Editions Gallimard, 1971.

———. *The Philosophy of Existentialism*. Secaucus, N.J.: Citadel Press, 1961.

May, Rollo. *Man's Search for Himself.* New York: W. W. Norton & Company, 1953.

Moeller, Charles. *Modern Mentality and Evangelization.* New York: Alba House. Vol. 2, *God,* 1967; *The Church,* 1968.

Muelder, Walter G. *Toward a Discipline of Social Ethics.* Boston: Boston University Press, 1972.

Padovano, Anthony T. *The Estranged God.* New York: Sheed & Ward, 1966.

Piaget, Jean. *Language and Thought of the Child.* 3rd ed. New York: Humanities Press, 1962.

Prick, J. J. G. *De Betenkenis Van Dr. A. A. A. Terruwe Voor De Psychiative.* Amsterdam: De Tijdstroom, 1972.

Reich, Charles. *The Greening of America: How the Youth Revolution Is Trying to Make America Liveable.* New York: Random House, 1970.

Riesman, David. *The Lonely Crowd: A Study of the Changing American Character.* Rev. ed. New Haven: Yale University Press, 1969.

Roberts, David E. *Existentialism and Religious Belief.* New York: Oxford University Press, 1959.

Teilhard de Chardin, Pierre. *The Future of Man.* New York: Harper & Row, 1964.

Terruwe, Anna A. *The Abode of Love.* Translated by Robert C. Ware. St. Meinrad, Ind.: Abbey Press, 1970.

Terruwe, Anna A., and Baars, Conrad W. *Loving and Curing the Neurotic.* New Rochelle, N. Y.: Arlington House, 1972.

Wright, John Cardinal. *The Church: Hope of the World.* Kenosha, Wis.: Prow Books, 1972.

INDEX

Acceptance, 33, 36
Adolescence, 31, 33, 36, 41
Affirmation, 14, 18, 71-76
Alfrink, Bernard Jan, 74
Algeria, 58-60, 63
Anxiety, 7, 41
Ashe, Ann, 19
Autonomy, 14-15, 32-33

Baars, Conrad, 18, 72
Baldwin, James, 46-47, 51
"Banking," 61
Behavior, 32
Black Americans, 46

Change, social, 22-24, 45, 62
Carmichael, Stokely, 46
Choice, 24
Christian, 15, 25, 69, 74, 75
Christianity, 67, 74, 75
Church, 25, 40, 69-70, 74
Communication, 23, 30
Community, 38, 62-63, 69
Cox, Harvey, 49
Crisis, 31

Denial, 71
Development, 11, 12, 13-14, 29-32

Education, 60-62

Environment, 11-12, 29, 32-33
Erikson, Erik, 29, 31, 40, 41
Exploitation, 45-47

Fanon, Frantz, 58
Fantasy, 28
Freedom, 29, 57, 74
Freire, Paulo, 57-58, 60-62

Genesis, 43-44, 65, 68
Goals, 32, 57

Healing, 13-14, 69, 72
House of Affirmation, 19

Identity
    crisis, 12, 22, 23, 28, 75
    definition, 27
    experimental, 36
    group, 29
    human, 17, 39
    personal, 13, 18, 22, 28-29, 30,
        32, 33, 51, 60
Ideology, 31-32, 41-42
Illich, Ivan, 60-61
Image, 28
Individuality, 13, 21, 22, 31, 35, 41,
    42, 63

Jesus, 24-25, 66-67, 69, 73

79

Jews, 39

Lambourne, R. A., 18

Marcel, Gabriel, 18, 50, 67, 68
Marxism, 42, 74
Mass production, 49-51, 53
Mass society, 51, 52, 53-54

Padovano, Anthony, 68
Parenteau, Ghislaine, 19
Peer group, 31-32, 33, 36-37, 40-41
Piaget, Jean, 29-31, 62
Polcino, Anna, 11-15, 18
Prejudice, 41
Pressure, 45, 51
Psychotheology, 13-15, 17-18, 24,
    65

Reich, Charles, 52-54, 60
Relationship, 24-33, passim, 39-40,
    43-44, 45, 46, 49-51, 53, 59,
    67, 68, 70

Revolution, 24, 43, 45, 60, 62
Riesman, David, 68

Self-awareness, 68
"Significant other," 72-73
Social behavior, 30
Social change, 18, 21-24, 45
Social group, 40
Social systems, 68-69, 71
Society, 11, 12, 21, 22, 24, 54, 73
Soviet Russia, 45-46

Technology, 22, 66-67
Terruwe, Anna, 18, 68, 72-73
Totality, 41
Traditions, 13, 39, 58
Trust, 33

Values, 18, 24, 39

Work, 32

Zacchaeus, 73